FOOTBALL WORLD
PLAYERS

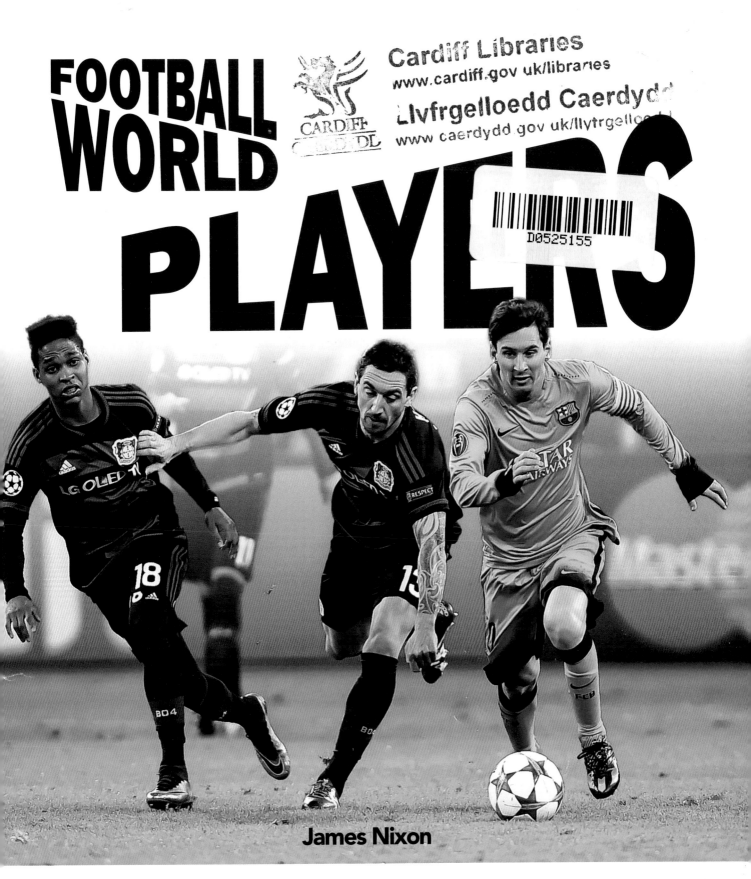

James Nixon

Franklin Watts
First published in Great Britain in 2017 by The Watts Publishing Group

Copyright © this edition The Watts Publishing Group, 2020

Credits
Editor: James Nixon
Design: Keith Williams, sprout.uk.com
Planning and production by Discovery Books Limited

Photo credits: Cover image: Alamy (GUIDO KIRCHNER/dpa).
Bigstock: pp. 4 (Maxisports), 8 bottom (Celso Pupo), 11 top (Celso Pupo), 12 middle (Maxisports), 12 bottom (bettorodrigues), 15 top (Celso Pupo), 15 bottom (katatonia82), 16 top (Maxisports), 17 top (Maxisports), 18 bottom (Maxisports), 20 top (Maxisports), 21 top (Celso Pupo), 21 bottom (hkratky), 24 top (sportsphotographer.eu) 25 bottom (Celso Pupo), 29 top (sportsphotographer.eu), 31 (katatonia82).
Getty Images: pp. 5 bottom (Dan Mullan/Stringer), 6 top (Manuel Queimadelos Alonso/Stringer), 9 bottom (JEFF PACHOUD/AFP), 14 top (Alex Broadway/Stringer), 19 top (Catherine Ivill – AMA), 19 bottom (Hector Vivas/STR), 22 bottom (Clive Brunskill), 24 bottom (John Peters), 25 top (GLYN KIRK/AFP).
Shutterstock: pp. 5 top (Marcos Mesa Sam Wordley), 6 bottom (Vlad1988), 7 top (Cristiano Barni), 7 bottom (Alizada Studios) 8 top (imagestockdesign), 9 top (MediaPictures.pl), 10 top (Fabrizio Andrea Bertani), 10 bottom (CosminIftode), 11 bottom (Fingerhut), 12 top (Marco Iacobucci EPP), 13 top (Marco Iacobucci EPP), 13 bottom (Alizada Studios), 14 bottom (mohsen nabil), 16 bottom (Vlad1988), 17 bottom (Marco Iacobucci EPP), 18 top (Marco Iacobucci EPP), 20 bottom (CosminIftode), 22 top (Anton_Ivanov), 23 top (Natursports), 23 bottom (Anton_Ivanov), 25 bottom (CosminIftode), 28 top-left (mr3002), 28 top-right (Mitch Gunn), 29 bottom (A.Ricardo).
Wikimedia: pp, 26 top (Agência Brasil Fotografias), 26 bottom (Chris Simpson), 27 top (joshjdss), 27 bottom (Pierre-Yves Beaudouin/Wikimedia Commons/CC BY-SA 3.0), 28 bottom (Agência Brasília).

ISBN: 978 1 4451 5577 7

Printed in Dubai

FSC
www.fsc.org

MIX
Paper from
responsible sources
FSC® C104740

Franklin Watts
An imprint of
Hachette Children's Group
Part of The Watts Publishing Group
Carmelite House
50 Victoria Embankment
London EC4Y 0DZ

An Hachette UK Company
www.hachette.co.uk

www.franklinwatts.co.uk

CONTENTS

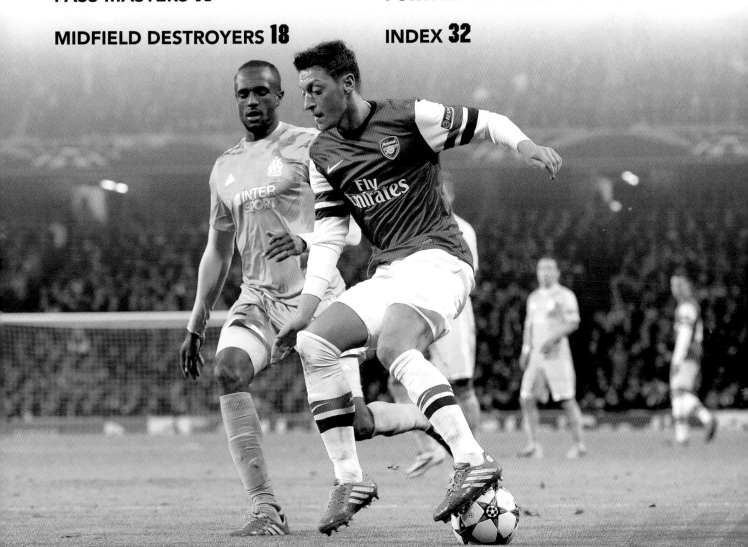

STARS OF THE GAME

The top footballers in the game come from all over the world. They display their talents while playing for the biggest clubs in major leagues. Some of today's footballers are so skilful that they can be placed among the greatest in the history of football.

Marvellous Messi

Lionel Messi from Argentina is definitely one of the all-time greats. There is no sight more terrifying to a defender than Messi dribbling at them at full speed. Messi is short for a footballer at just 1.7 metres high. Yet his low **centre of gravity**, plus his quick feet, let him twist, turn and dart past defenders. With his precise passing and finishing, Messi creates and scores an astonishing number of goals.

Messi's skills have helped Spanish club Barcelona become one of the most successful teams in the world in recent years. The Ballon d'Or award, given to the best player in world football, has been won by Messi five times in the last ten years.

FLASH FACT

Lionel Messi holds the record for the most goals scored in a football season (73) and a calendar year (91).

 ## Stat Tracker

	Games played	Goals
Lionel Messi		
Barcelona	687	603
Argentina	131	67
Cristiano Ronaldo		
Juventus	43	28
Portugal	158	88
Gareth Bale		
Real Madrid	231	102
Wales	77	31

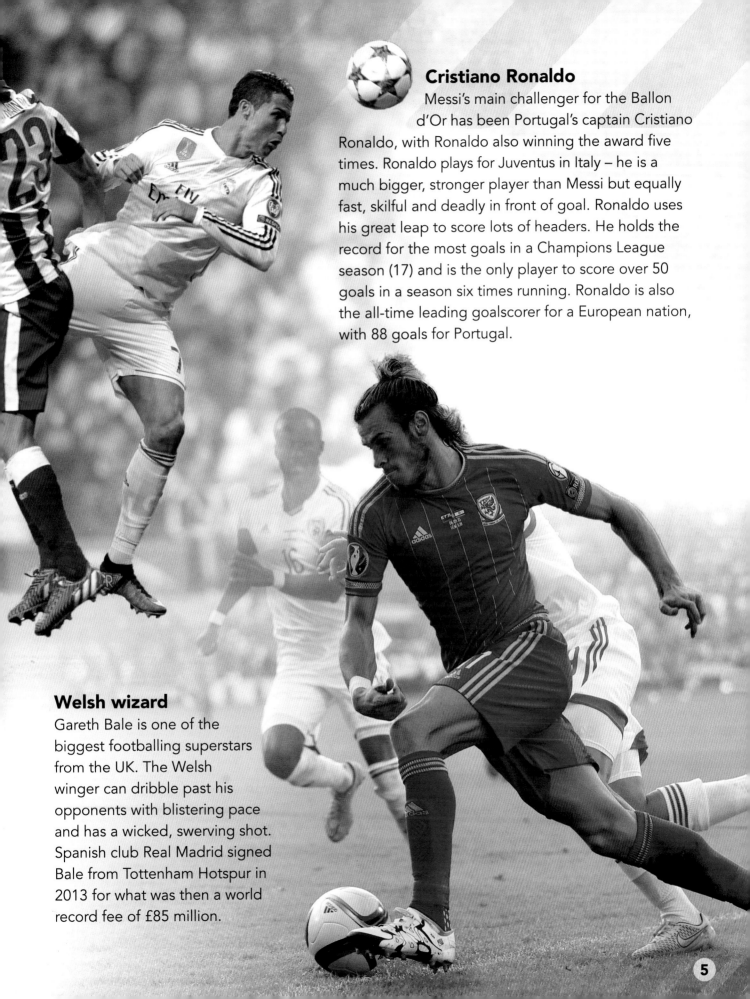

Cristiano Ronaldo

Messi's main challenger for the Ballon d'Or has been Portugal's captain Cristiano Ronaldo, with Ronaldo also winning the award five times. Ronaldo plays for Juventus in Italy – he is a much bigger, stronger player than Messi but equally fast, skilful and deadly in front of goal. Ronaldo uses his great leap to score lots of headers. He holds the record for the most goals in a Champions League season (17) and is the only player to score over 50 goals in a season six times running. Ronaldo is also the all-time leading goalscorer for a European nation, with 88 goals for Portugal.

Welsh wizard

Gareth Bale is one of the biggest footballing superstars from the UK. The Welsh winger can dribble past his opponents with blistering pace and has a wicked, swerving shot. Spanish club Real Madrid signed Bale from Tottenham Hotspur in 2013 for what was then a world record fee of £85 million.

SKILL PLAYERS

The most skilled footballers can get the crowd in the stadium out of their seats. They can mesmerise defenders with their dribbles and skills. These players make the difference – in an instant they can turn a game heading for a 0-0 draw into a victory for their team.

Neymar

Brazilian attacker Neymar is one of the most exciting players in world football. Known for his dribbling, finishing and ability with both feet, Neymar's performances are often incredible and hugely entertaining. He has all the tricks in the book, from **dummies** and **stepovers** to fool defenders, to backheels and flicks that create chances for his teammates. In 2016, he scored the winning **penalty** to earn Brazil the Olympic gold medal.

FLASH FACT

In 2017, Neymar became the most expensive footballer ever when French club Paris Saint-Germain (PSG) bought him from Barcelona for £200 million!

Watch out – Hazard!

Belgium forward Eden Hazard is one of the most dangerous attackers when running at defenders. Hazard's close control at pace often makes it appear as if the ball is glued to his foot. This lets him go past his opponent in even the tightest of spots. Real Madrid signed Hazard from Chelsea in 2019 for a fee that could rise to £150 million.

Free kick king

Bosnian midfielder Miralem Pjanić is one of the most technically gifted footballers in the world. His quick feet, close control and clever touches are a joy to watch. Dubbed the 'Little Prince', Pjanić was signed by Italian giants Juventus in 2016. Pjanić is also considered by some to be the world's best free-kick taker. He is able to curl the ball over a defensive wall and into the net with incredible accuracy.

Stat Tracker

	Games played	Goals
Neymar		
PSG	58	51
Brazil	97	60
Eden Hazard		
Chelsea	352	110
Belgium	102	30
Miralem Pjanić		
Juventus	135	19
Bosnia	86	13
Mohamed Salah		
Liverpool	104	71
Egypt	62	39

Marvellous Mo

Liverpool and Egyptian attacker Mohamed Salah has explosive speed and dribbling skills. He won the Premier League **Golden Boot** in 2018 and 2019. In 2018, he scored a league record 32 goals in 36 games. Salah was also voted African Footballer of the Year in 2018 and 2019.

PURE GOALSCORERS

Goals win football matches, so high-scoring strikers are in constant demand. The very best finishers keep cool in that moment of pressure and are deadly accurate.

Super Suárez

Luis Suárez from Uruguay is one of the most **prolific** strikers in football history. He has scored heaps of goals at all the clubs he has played for. The European **Golden Boot** prize is given to Europe's leading league goalscorer. Suárez has won this twice, while at Liverpool in 2014 and at Barcelona in 2016. His trickery and direct running often put Suárez in positions to score. His favourite move is to **nutmeg** the defender to get past them.

Sergio Agüero

Argentina and Manchester City striker Sergio Agüero can terrorise defenders like few others. Agüero has one of the highest goals-per-minute ratio in the history of the Premier League. His razor-sharp movement and supreme strength and balance can leave opponents for dead. Agüero can strike the ball powerfully with both feet and can finish well from inside and outside the penalty box.

FLASH FACT

In 2003, Sergio Agüero became the youngest player to compete in Argentina's top league. He was aged just 15 years and 35 days!

Robert Lewandowski

Poland captain Robert Lewandowski is one of today's most impressive finishers. Starring for Bayern Munich in the German Bundesliga, Lewandowski won the top scorer prize for the fourth time in 2019. Amazingly, in 2015, with his side 1-0 down to Wolfsburg, Lewandowski came on as substitute and scored five goals in the space of nine minutes! For this achievement Lewandowski was awarded four different Guiness World Records.

Alexandre Lacazette

French striker Alexandre Lacazette was already a star for Lyon, scoring 27 goals in 33 appearances in 2015 before Arsenal snapped him up for £46.5 million. He can score all types of goals, including **one-on-ones**, volleys and long shots. In 2019, he was voted Arsenal's 'Player of the Year' by club supporters.

Stat Tracker

	Games played	Goals
Luis Suárez Barcelona Uruguay	247 107	177 56
Sergio Agüero Manchester City Argentina	337 89	231 39
Robert Lewandowski Bayern Munich Poland	242 106	191 57
Alexandre Lacazette Arsenal France	88 16	36 3

TARGETMEN

As well as scoring goals, strikers that play as targetmen have the job of winning long balls and holding on to the ball while their teammates advance up the pitch. Each of these four players make perfect targets.

Mauro Icardi

Italian striker Mauro Icardi doesn't give defenders a moment's peace. His determination to chase down long balls and his intelligent movement in the penalty box put the opposition under constant pressure. Icardi doesn't need many chances to score and is a cool finisher with both his head and feet. Playing for Inter Milan in Italy he scored over 100 goals in five seasons, and was the top scorer and Footballer of the Year in the Serie A league in 2018.

Harry Kane

This England and Tottenham Hotspur striker has all the top targetman skills. He is tall so he can challenge for long aerial balls, and his good technique means he can control passes and hold on to the ball while he is being marked. Kane's powerful and accurate shooting helped him win the Premier League Golden Boot in both 2016 and 2017, as well as the Golden Boot at the World Cup in 2018.

FLASH FACT

*In 2015, Harry Kane made his England **debut** against Lithuania and scored with a header after just 80 seconds!*

Romelu Lukaku

Ex-Manchester United and Belgium international Romelu Lukaku is the classic big and strong targetman. With his back to defenders, he has the ability to use his muscle to spin away from them towards goal. Lukaku is one of only five players in history to score 50 Premier League goals before his 23rd birthday. He joined Italian giants Inter Milan for a cool £74 million in August 2019.

Stat Tracker

	Games played	Goals
Mauro Icardi Inter Milan Argentina	219 8	124 1
Harry Kane Tottenham Hotspur England	253 39	164 22
Romelu Lukaku Manchester United Belgium	96 81	42 48
Pierre-Emerick Aubameyang Arsenal Gabon	65 59	41 24

Pierre-Emerick Aubameyang

Pierre-Emerick Aubameyang is one of the most dangerous strikers in world football. He plays for the Gabon national team and Arsenal. Known for his electric speed, he can beat defenders to long passes over the top and through the back line. In the 2016/2017 season he scored 40 goals in 46 games for Borussia Dortmund in Germany. He joined Arsenal the next season for a club-record £56 million and has continued his goalscoring form.

NUMBER TENS

The number ten shirt is often worn by the deeper-lying support striker or the central attacking midfielder. 'Number ten' has since become the name for this position between midfield and attack. The job of a number ten is to create goals as well as score them.

Kevin De Bruyne

Belgian Kevin De Bruyne is a master in the number ten role. He was signed by Manchester City in 2015 for £54 million. De Bruyne **assists** many goals with his intelligent and pinpoint passing that can split open defences. He scores plenty too, including some stunning strikes from outside the box. He was named Manchester City's Player of the Year in 2018.

Star of the Euros

Antoine Griezmann has been a scoring sensation for France and Spanish club Atlético Madrid. Griezmann has pace, energy, clever movement and can link up play between midfielders and attackers. On top of this, he takes **set pieces** and can finish well with his feet as well as his head! In 2018, France won the World Cup and Griezmann was awarded Man of the Match in the final. Griezmann swopped Atlético for Spanish giants Barcelona in 2019.

FLASH FACT

The Golden Boot winner at the 2014 World Cup was Colombian and Real Madrid number ten James Rodríguez. He scored six goals in five games.

Dele Alli

Number tens can be hard for opponents to mark because they drift about in the space between midfield and attack. There is no greater example of this than Tottenham Hotspur and England star Dele Alli. Alli uses his ability to find space in and around the penalty box to consistently score and create goals. According to his club manager Mauricio Pochettino, Alli looks like a striker in the box, but plays like a midfielder outside it. That is the perfect mix for a number ten.

Stat Tracker

	Games played	Goals
Kevin De Bruyne Manchester City Belgium	173 70	40 16
Antoine Griezmann Atlético Madrid France	257 70	133 29
Dele Alli Tottenham Hotspur England	184 37	53 3
Philippe Coutinho Barcelona Brazil	75 50	21 16

Little Magician

Sometimes nicknamed the Little Magician, Brazilian Philippe Coutinho has special magic in his feet. His mazy dribbles, **vision** and imagination create goalscoring chance after chance. He sees passes other players wouldn't. Coutinho is also famous for bending long-range strikes into the top corner of the net. Barcelona bought him from Liverpool for a whopping £142 million in 2018.

TRICKY WINGERS

Wingers play and attack down the sides of the pitch. The best wingers use pace and trickery to get past their opponents and can deliver dangerous crosses into the box.

Riyad Mahrez

Algerian winger Riyad Mahrez played a key role in Leicester City's shock Premier League win in 2016. Before the season, Leicester were given a one in 5,000 chance of winning! Mahrez ended up being voted the **PFA** Player's Player of the Year. Dribbling mainly with his left foot, Mahrez can effortlessly dodge past defenders and unleash a lethal, curling shot. He joined Manchester City in July 2018 and won a second Premier League title with them!

⚽ Stat Tracker

	Games played	Goals
Riyad Mahrez Manchester City Algeria	44 43	12 10
Sadio Mané Liverpool Senegal	123 60	59 16
Alexis Sánchez Manchester Utd Chile	45 124	5 41
Raheem Sterling Manchester City England	191 51	69 8

Sadio Mané

Mané, from Senegal, has lightning acceleration and eye for the goal that terrifies defenders. The agile winger helped Liverpool become champions of Europe when they won the Champions League in 2019. He scored 22 Premier League goals in the 2018/2019 season, sharing the Golden Boot with his teammate Mohamed Salah and Pierre-Emerick Aubameyang.

Alexis Sánchez

Winger Alexis Sánchez (left) has helped his nation Chile win two **Copa América** championships. Quick, agile, and with huge amounts of flair, Sánchez can skip past opponents. Like many top wingers, Sánchez has the **work rate** and energy to track back and help his defence, too. In 2019, Sánchez joined Inter Milan on loan from Manchester United.

FLASH FACT

*In Chile's 2016 Copa América semi-final victory over Colombia, Alexis Sánchez became the first Chilean outfield player to reach 100 **caps**.*

Raheem Sterling

Manchester City signed winger Raheem Sterling from Liverpool for £49 million in 2015. This was then the highest **transfer** fee ever paid for an English player. The year before Sterling had won the Golden Boy award, given to the best under-21 player in Europe. Sterling is a small, pacy winger who has the craft and dribbling skills to unlock any defence. He has been a key player in Manchester City's Premier League titles in 2018 and 2019, scoring 35 times.

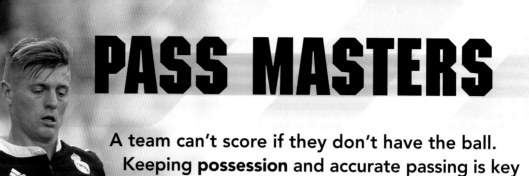

PASS MASTERS

A team can't score if they don't have the ball. Keeping **possession** and accurate passing is key to winning football matches. Here are some of the top players that make their teams tick.

Toni Kroos

German and Real Madrid midfielder Toni Kroos is known for his phenomenal passing accuracy. Playmakers like Kroos are fluent in receiving and passing the ball and make the game look easy. He helped Real Madrid win three Champions League titles in a row between 2016 and 2018. Kroos also sets up many goals with his superb vision and set pieces. He recorded the highest number of assists in the 2014 World Cup to help Germany win the trophy.

FLASH FACT

In 2014, Toni Kroos became the first player born in the former country of **East Germany** *to win a World Cup.*

Mini maestro

Italian international Marco Verratti stands at just 1.65 metres tall, yet he is one of the finest midfielders in the world. Verratti is super-confident on the ball and very rarely gives it away. His close ball control and low centre of gravity help him hold on to possession in tight spaces. Verratti controls the tempo of his side's play. He is a master of long and short passing and can play a killer final pass to the strikers too. Since he joined French club Paris Saint-Germain in 2012, his team have won six French league titles in a row.

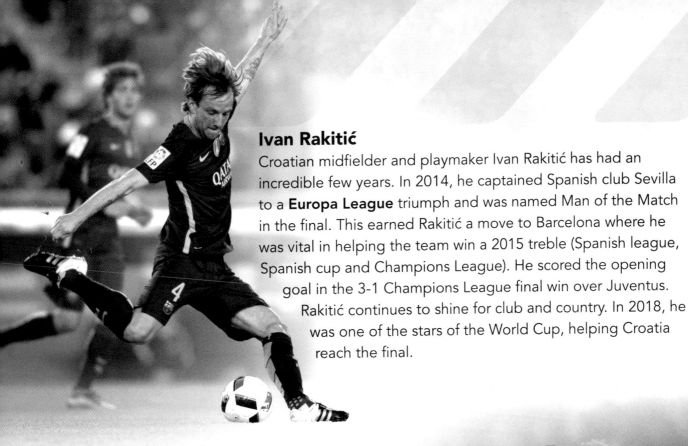

Ivan Rakitić

Croatian midfielder and playmaker Ivan Rakitić has had an incredible few years. In 2014, he captained Spanish club Sevilla to a **Europa League** triumph and was named Man of the Match in the final. This earned Rakitić a move to Barcelona where he was vital in helping the team win a 2015 treble (Spanish league, Spanish cup and Champions League). He scored the opening goal in the 3-1 Champions League final win over Juventus. Rakitić continues to shine for club and country. In 2018, he was one of the stars of the World Cup, helping Croatia reach the final.

Leonardo Bonucci

It is not just midfielders that need to be good at passing. Italian defender Leonardo Bonucci is an expert at directing play from the back with precise passing. Bonucci is a cool defender who doesn't panic with the ball at his feet. In fact he has the ability to launch attacks with his long passes. Bonucci has won seven Serie A league titles with Juventus since 2012!

 Stat Tracker

	Games played	Goals
Toni Kroos Real Madrid Germany	233 92	13 14
Marco Verratti Paris Saint-Germain Italy	277 33	9 3
Ivan Rakitić Barcelona Croatia	268 104	35 15
Leonardo Bonucci Juventus Italy	360 89	22 7

MIDFIELD DESTROYERS

Successful teams more often than not win the midfield battle. They have midfielders that are energetic, strong and tough in the tackle. These players protect their team's defence and help to kickstart attacks.

Paul Pogba

French star Paul Pogba was signed by Manchester United from Juventus in 2016 for what was then a world record transfer fee of £89 million. Pogba is a **commanding** midfielder – with his height and long legs, he has the stamina and skill of a **box-to-box midfielder.** He tackles and blocks shots in defence, but can also power forward into his opponent's box to score. What distinguishes Pogba are his ball skills – he can swiftly change play from defence to attack. Pogba scored the crucial third goal for France in the 2018 World Cup final as his side defeated Croatia 4-2.

FLASH FACT

Paul Pogba won the Best Young Player award at the 2014 World Cup. The prize is contested between players at the tournament aged 21 or under.

Busy Busquets

Sergio Busquets is the quiet hero of the Spain and Barcelona team. He may not have the flashy skills of the big names, but he is just as important. Busquets is the master of positioning, always in place to **intercept** an attack and shield his defence. And when he wins the ball, he rarely loses possession.

The interceptor

N'Golo Kanté was one of the biggest stars in Leicester City's 2016 Premier League fairytale. Chelsea signed him the following summer for £32 million. Despite measuring just 1.69 metres Kanté is a true midfield destroyer. His tackling is hard and well timed, but he is also expert at breaking down opponents' attacks by making interceptions. The secret to this skill is his ability to read the game, which means he can predict what his opponents will do next. Kanté is also comfortable bursting forward with the ball to put the opposition's defence under pressure.

The warrior

Chilean international Arturo Vidal (below right) is a complete midfielder, known for his tackling, passing and powerful shots from distance. His physical and aggressive style of play earned him the nickname 'The Warrior'. After winning three Bundesliga titles in a row with Bayern Munich he joined Barcelona in 2018.

Stat Tracker

	Games played	Goals
Paul Pogba		
Manchester United	135	31
France	69	10
Sergio Busquets		
Barcelona	536	13
Spain	112	2
N'Golo Kanté		
Chelsea	142	8
France	38	1
Arturo Vidal		
Barcelona	53	3
Chile	105	26

FLYING FULL BACKS

Full backs play either side of the central defenders. The best full backs are just as skilled in attacking as defending. To sprint up and down the pitch, these players need good pace and stamina.

Jordi Alba

Spain's Jordi Alba is Barcelona's speedy left back. Attacking wingers up against Alba usually find themselves running backwards chasing Alba instead! Alba is skilful enough to play as a winger himself. In 2016, he scored the crucial goal in extra time as Barcelona beat Sevilla to win the Spanish cup.

Speedy Walker

Kyle Walker (below left) is one of the game's finest. The powerful England player just loves to burst down the right touchline and swing crosses into the opposition's box. Defensively he has the pace to track back and make vital tackles. In 2017, Manchester City signed Walker from Tottenham Hotspur for £50 million, making him one of the most expensive defenders in the world.

Stat Tracker

	Games played	Goals
Jordi Alba Barcelona Spain	300 67	15 8
Kyle Walker Manchester City England	100 48	2 0
Marcelo Real Madrid Brazil	486 58	36 6
David Alaba Bayern Munich Austria	344 64	29 13

Marcelo

Brazilian and Real Madrid left back Marcelo is without question the most skilful defender in the world today. Marcelo is able to dribble past player after player, yet he combines this attacking flair with defensive steel. His skills with both feet make him dangerous. He can dart down the left and cross or cut inside and unleash a shot with his right foot.

David Alaba

Bayern Munich left back David Alaba has been a revelation for the German champions. Alaba has the speed to charge into space but also to recover when his team's attack fizzles out. He has such great passing and shooting ability that his country Austria sometimes uses Alaba as a number ten and the driving force behind their attacks!

FLASH FACT

David Alaba was Austrian Footballer of the Year for five years running between 2011 and 2015 and gained the record of Austria's youngest ever capped player when he was 17.

TOP DEFENDERS

Stopping goals is just as important as scoring them. A defender's job is to block shots, tackle, win headers and mark forwards. Here are some of the best in the business.

A powerhouse

Kalidou Koulibaly (right) is one of the strongest and toughest defenders in the world. The powerhouse from Senegal is dominant in the air and makes crunching tackles. His pace helps him close down attackers in a flash. Koulibaly plays his club football for Napoli in Italy, where fans have nicknamed him The Wall because attackers can't get past him. Whoever signs him next will surely have to pay big money.

Solid as Stones

In 2016, at the age of 22, England defender John Stones moved from Everton to Manchester City for a hefty £47.5 million. Manchester City signed Stones for his calmness and ability to pass and move his way out of danger. Commanding in the air and on the ground, Stones has everything it takes to become one of the game's greats.

FLASH FACT

Shane Duffy, the Brighton & Hove Albion player, topped the Premier League charts for goals from a defender (5) and clearances made (243) in the 2018/2019 season.

Raphaël Varane

Real Madrid defender Raphaël Varane was a key part of France's World Cup-winning side in 2018. He has a remarkable ability to read the game and can put himself in the right position, anticipate danger and make vital challenges and interceptions. When he finds himself out of position, Varane can use his searing pace and execute a perfect sliding tackle. When he was 22 Varane became the youngest player ever to captain France.

Dutch master

The Netherlands captain Virgil van Dijk briefly became the world's most expensive defender in 2018 when he joined Liverpool from Southampton for £75 million. Van Dijk's height and strength, combined with good technique and passing, has made him one of the game's most complete defenders. In 2019, Van Dijk was voted Premier League Player of the Season and was named Man of the Match in Liverpool's Champions League final victory.

⚽ Stat Tracker

	Games played	Goals
Kalidou Koulibaly Napoli Senegal	212 32	10 0
John Stones Manchester City England	109 38	5 2
Raphaël Varane Real Madrid France	276 58	12 4
Virgil van Dijk Liverpool Netherlands	72 28	7 4

GOALKEEPERS

The greatest goalkeepers can produce heroic and spellbinding saves to help their teams win any match. These players must be supremely **agile** and athletic.

Sweeper keeper

Bayern Munich goalkeeper Manuel Neuer is regarded as one of the best goalkeepers of all time. Neuer is a fantastic shot-stopper and commands his area well by punching away and catching crosses. He also likes to rush outside his penalty box and beat strikers to the ball. Neuer is a bit like an 11th outfield player, spraying passes around the pitch. This style of play has led him to be described as a 'sweeper keeper'. As captain of Germany he won the 2014 World Cup and was awarded the **Golden Glove** for the best goalkeeper of the tournament.

FLASH FACT

Between 2013 and 2015, Manuel Neuer won the IFFHS World's Best Goalkeeper award three years running!

David De Gea

Spanish goalkeeper David De Gea was Manchester United's Player of the Year between 2014 and 2016, and again in 2018. In 2018, he won the award for the Premier League Save of the Season, given by the *Match of the Day* TV programme, for the fifth season running. De Gea's **reflexes** are outstanding, and help him deliver impossible-looking saves.

Thibaut Courtois

Belgian goalkeeper Thibaut Courtois stands 1.99 metres high and is a daunting figure in goal for strikers to face. In 2017, he helped Chelsea win the Premier League, winning the prize for keeping the most **clean sheets** (16). At the 2018 World Cup, Belgium made the semi-finals. Courtouis made more saves than any other keeper in the tournament and was awarded the Golden Glove. After the World Cup he signed for Real Madrid.

Marc-André Ter Stegen

Barcelona and German shot-stopper Marc-André Ter Stegen is arguably the best goalkeeper in the world right now. He possesses cat-like agility and lightning reflexes, and is effective at commanding and organising his defenders. He will surely be challenging Manuel Neuer for the German number-one shirt soon.

WOMEN'S FOOTBALL

Women's football is rapidly growing in popularity. Here are some of the best players on the planet today.

Magnificent Marta

Brazilian Marta is considered the best female player of all time. Marta is a classic number ten, known for her creativity, flair and goalscoring. She is small and quick, yet strong and tenacious. Marta also has quick feet and remarkable skill on the ball, which allows her to dribble at pace. Between 2006 and 2018 she won FIFA World Player of the Year a record six times.

FLASH FACT

Marta holds the record for the most goals scored at FIFA Women's World Cup tournaments. She has found the net 17 times.

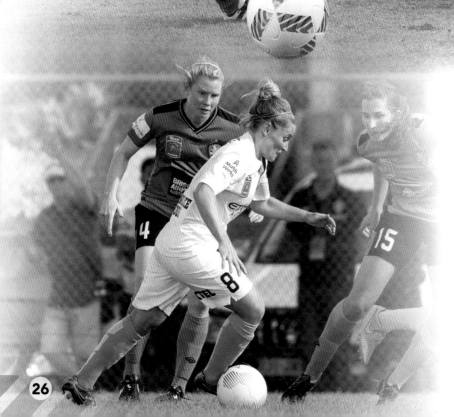

Kim Little

Scottish midfielder Kim Little is a scoring sensation from midfield. Little is always looking to be positive and make forward runs. Between 2009 and 2012 she was part of the Arsenal side that won four English league titles. In 2016, she was named BBC Women's Footballer of the Year, and in 2019 she helped Arsenal win the league title again.

Alex Morgan

American Alex Morgan (left) is one of the most prolific strikers in women's football. Morgan has the speed to outrun defenders and the finishing skill to outwit goalkeepers. In 2018, Morgan scored 18 goals in just 19 appearances for the United States national team.

Steph Houghton

England captain and Manchester City defender Steph Houghton (right) has made over 100 appearances for her country. In the 2012 Summer Olympics Houghton played for the Great Britain side and scored in all three group games. Her performances led her to be named the 'left back of the tournament'. Houghton has everything it takes to be a world-class defender – she can head and tackle, but also has that touch of skill and flair to play out from the back.

Amandine Henry

French player Amandine Henry, who plays for Lyon, is perhaps the best midfielder in the women's game today. In 2015, 2016 and 2018 she placed in the top three for the UEFA Best Women's Player in Europe award.

⚽ Stat Tracker

	Games played	Goals
Marta Brazil	146	113
Alex Morgan USA	164	106
Amandine Henry France	83	11
Steph Houghton England	106	12
Kim Little Scotland	135	54

STARS OF THE FUTURE

These are the top young talents that have the potential to be the megastars of the future.

Man U double-act

Manchester United's future looks very bright. In Anthony Martial (right) and Marcus Rashford (left) they have two forwards who could dominate the league for years to come.

Martial was signed from French club Monaco in 2015 for a fee that could rise to £57.6 million. In the same year Martial won the Golden Boy award for the best under-21 player in Europe. He has the speed, skill and calmness in front of goal that gives defences nightmares.

Rashford is a couple of years younger than Martial but equally **dynamic** and dangerous. In 2016, aged just 18, Rashford became the youngest player ever to score on his debut for England.

Gabriel Jesus

In 2017, Manchester City signed hot prospect and Brazilian forward Gabriel Jesus for a total fee of £31 million. In 2015, Jesus had helped his club Palmeiras win the Copa do Brasil knockout cup and was voted the best newcomer in the Brazilian league. Known for his pace, finishing and work rate, Jesus sensationally scored two goals and made an assist on his Brazil debut in 2016.

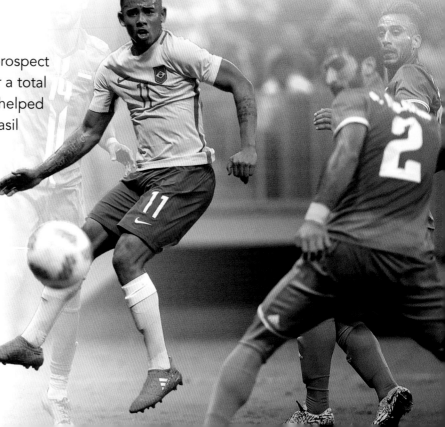

Kingsley Coman

French winger Kingsley Coman is one of the most promising young players of his generation. In 2015, Coman joined German giants Bayern Munich. In the 2016 German Cup final, he won his eighth club trophy before his 20th birthday! Coman is a brilliant dribbler who has the tricks and vision to beat defenders and set up goals.

⚽ Stat Tracker

	Games played	Goals
Anthony Martial		
Manchester United	174	48
France	18	1
Marcus Rashford		
Manchester United	170	45
England	32	7
Gabriel Jesus		
Manchester City	99	45
Brazil	30	16
Kingsley Coman		
Bayern Munich	123	25
France	16	1
Kylian Mbappé		
Paris Saint-Germain	87	60
France	33	13

FLASH FACT

Kylian Mbappé became the most expensive teenager ever signed when Paris Saint-Germain paid Monaco £166 million for him!

World Cup winner

Kylian Mbappé is already a footballing megastar. At just 19 years old, Mbappé scored a goal in the 2018 World Cup final and a total of four in the tournament as his team France were crowned champions. Mbappé's quick feet and close control, combined with his outstanding pace and strength, is frightening. He also possesses a lethal shot. In the 2018/2019 season, he scored 33 goals in 29 league games for PSG, and was the French Ligue 1's top scorer and Player of the Year.

GLOSSARY

agile able to move quickly and easily

assist a pass from which a teammate scores

box-to-box midfielder an energetic midfielder who helps the team's attack and defence equally

cap appearance for the national team

centre of gravity the central part of the body from which weight takes effect

clean sheet when a goalkeeper concedes no goals in a game

commanding the ability to dominate

Copa América a major tournament contested by national sides from South America

debut first appearance for a new team

dummy a pretend kick (plural: dummies)

dynamic highly active and energetic

East Germany a former country that reunited with West Germany in 1990 to form present-day Germany

Europa League a European club competition for teams that have finished close to the top of their national league

Golden Boot an award given to the top scorer in a competition

Golden Glove an award given to the goalkeeper with the most clean sheets in a competition

intercept stop an opponent's pass

loan when a club borrows a player from another club for a set time

nutmeg kick the ball through the opponent's legs

one-on-one a chance for the striker to score, where they just have the goalkeeper to beat

penalty a free shot from the penalty spot (11 metres from goal) with just the goalkeeper to beat

PFA stands for the Players' Football Association, which is a union of professional footballers

possession if a team or player has control of the ball they are in possession

prolific producing many goals

reflexes quick reactions to a moving ball

set piece when the ball is kicked back into play, such as from a corner or free kick

stepover a sharp movement of the leg over the ball, instead of kicking it, to fool the defender

transfer when a player moves from one club to another

vision the ability to see a good pass

work rate the amount of effort a player puts in

FURTHER INFORMATION

BOOKS

EDGE: Sporting Heroes series,
Roy Apps, Franklin Watts, 2017

Greatest Players (Planet Football),
Clive Gifford, Wayland, 2017

*Messi, Superstar: His Records,
His Life, His Epic Awesomeness*,
Duo Press LLC, 2016

Stars of All Time (World Soccer Legends),
Illusi Jokulsson, Abbeville Kids, 2017

The Ultimate Fan Book series,
Carlton Books, 2017

WEBSITES

www.fourfourtwo.com/features/
On this site you can find a list of the top 100
footballers in the world today.

www.footballsgreatest.weebly.com
Find out information about the greatest
footballers of all time.

www.youtube.com/watch?v=rA1102ZzprY
Video footage of 20 of the greatest
footballers in history.

www.premierleague.com/players
Find out the stats for any Premier
League player.

INDEX